# Days of Laughter

by J.R. Singh

# Preface

**Days of Laughter** is an effort to preserve some of the childhood experiences of many who lived in Guyana during the 1950s and 60s.

While this book is intended to make you smile and reflect on some of the simple joys in life, it is also a gentle reminder of some of the games children played in Guyana, the stories they listened to and the toys they made. In an effort to preserve what many have experienced while growing up in Guyana, this simple story takes account of some well-liked birds, popular individuals in certain villages, some notable places to visit, as well as common Guyanese Creole to remind us of our homeland.

# Days of Laughter

ISBN 978-0-9682461-2-2


Bluetree Publishing, Canada

# Days of Laughter

Today, a warm, sunny day in 1968, gives me great joy as a fifteen-year-old to look back at the childhood experiences of an earlier period and to link them together in this simple story.

*****

September of 1958 marked the beginning of my first school term in kindergarten, and my mother had to drag me by the hand to take me there. I was five years old and terrified at the thought of going to school, after being told several times by my older cousins that teachers would spank me if I were late or did not do my homework.

After my mother took me to school and then hurriedly left to go to work, I began to cry so loud that the headmistress came in a hurry to see what was wrong with me. Seconds later, my tears ended abruptly when she shouted harshly at me to stop crying. From the moment I saw her bend a "wild cane" across her broad shoulders and say, "I'm going to cut your little ass if you don't stop crying," I immediately lowered my head and kept quiet. With a grim face, the headmistress grabbed my hand and walked with me to a classroom that was filled with children my age. She introduced me to a middle-aged woman with broad hips named Mary Wilcox, saying that she would be my teacher.

Fortunately, by the end of the day, school turned out to be better than I thought. It was fun when Miss Mary taught the class the nursery rhyme "Humpty Dumpty." To amuse us while we recited the rhyme, she got one boy to sit on a chair and then pretend that he had fallen off his chair, while a few of us gathered around to pick him up. Soon, I became friends with a number of young boys and girls who were eager to play with me.

On my second day at school, I heard for the first time an amusing playgroup rhyme that was often said by a number of children when teacher Mary was not around. It seemed that they had made up this rhyme, and after listening to it day after day, I soon memorized it in its entirety.

After a week at school, my father called me over late one evening and asked me to tell him some of the things I had learned in school. Unfortunately, I was so absorbed with play that I could only recite a small part of the nursery rhyme "Humpty Dumpty." As I remained silent and scratched my head to think, my Aunty Nelly, who was my mother's sister from the island of Leguan, pleaded with me not to be shy, but to say whatever I was taught in school. It was not until my father suddenly yelled at me to speak up, that the rhyme I was taught by my friends at school suddenly came to mind. I then said, "When ah was small, ah had no sense, meh mudda buy ah guitar fuh eighteen cents. Now ah could play it ting ah ling ling, nobody could beat meh fuh sing." Looking at my father with his mouth open and in shock, I instantly realized that what I had said was totally unacceptable. When the expression on his face turned grim, I immediately sensed that he was going to strike me, so I quickly lifted up Aunty Nelly's frock (dress) and hid under it. As my dad repeatedly yelled at me to come out, my aunt pleaded with him not to hurt me.

Later when my father had calmed down, and had gone to sit on a reclining "Berbice" chair in our living room, I quietly crept out from under Aunty Nelly's dress and whispered in her ear, "Antie Nelly, ah see plenty hairs pon yuh legs." Embarrassed, she slapped me on the cheek and yelled, "Yuh chupidee bai! Gwhan dah side!" When my father heard her tell me that I was foolish and to go away, he got angry. Seeing me holding my cheek with a sad expression on my face, he repeatedly asked my aunt what her reason was for striking me. When Aunty Nelly did not utter a single word, I guessed that she was very embarrassed by what I had said. As I pouted and rubbed my eyes, my father questioned me about what I had said to make my aunt so upset. But I chose to remain silent, fearing that if I spoke the truth, Aunty Nelly would slap me a second time. By this time, my grandfather, who had been sitting in his room and getting annoyed by the yelling in the house, slowly came out twirling his long, black mustache, and demanded that Aunty Nelly and my dad stop quarreling. I must say that he was the central figure in the house and, within minutes, he settled their dispute.

My grandfather was a well-known man in Kitty village where I grew up, for he was a retired police detective. I remember him as a slick dresser, especially when he attended horse racing at Durban Park, wearing a suit and carrying a cigar. Like most other families of East Indian descent at the time, my grandfather enjoyed living among his daughters and his sons with their wives and children in the same house. There were twenty-two of us living in a four-bedroom house that had only two outdoor latrines and an external hut to shower in.

Living with a large number of relatives made these the happiest days of my life. Even though there was no television, you could be sure that, during the course of the day, you were likely to witness more than one amusing incident to make you laugh or smile. Even if there was nothing to laugh about in your home, you just had to look out of your window to be entertained either by a drunk man singing in the street, children playing in trenches, a mule running wildly down the road, or two neighbors quarreling over trivial matters. If this were not enough to amuse you, then you would definitely smile at a young boy pulling a donkey's tail and trying to avoid being kicked, or a couple of young girls running around plants, chasing butterflies. It amused me at age five to see at times some boys my age or a little younger being yelled at by adults when they were caught with their pants down in a contest to see who could pee the farthest.

Though my parents as well as other families in our area did not spend a great deal of time with their children because of the long hours they worked, it never dawned in our minds to complain about not getting enough attention from our parents. With the majority of us having our grandparents, as well as cousins and friends to play with, there was never a dull moment.

I recall my mother having to wake up about 4:00 a.m. from Monday to Friday each week to prepare meals, and to hand wash our clothes before going to work. Returning from work each day, she had to go to a marketplace to buy fresh meat, fish or vegetables, as in those days not all families could afford to have a refrigerator. Aside from this, it was a joy for my cousins and me to greet our parents when they came home from work, for almost every day our parents would give us one cent to buy a candy or a cake called "sweet bread."

Many women who stayed at home to raise their children had an enormous amount of household tasks to do. It was common to see some of them going from one chore to the next — cooking, washing, ironing, fetching water, cutting wood, going to the local marketplace, and even taking care of the vegetable garden in their yard.

From a tender age, my grandparents, aunts and uncles, as well as our neighbors, were the ones who now and again kept a watchful eye on me when my parents were not around. They were concerned about my safety, for if I were seen playing too far away from home, they would order me to go home immediately. From a young age it was instilled in me to obey them, for in those days most parents put a great deal of emphasis on respect for our elders, parents, teachers and neighbors.

The day after the incident with Aunty Nelly, I saw

her peeling the skin off a half-ripe mango called "buxton spice." When she began to rub salt and pepper on the mango, my lips became wet with saliva, and I could not resist asking her for a piece of it. With a glare, she grabbed my hand and drew me close to her. In a coarse voice she said, "Ah still vex wid yuh! Ah hope yuh staan easy an' yuh nah tell nobody, eh?" She meant that she was still angry with me and hoped that I had not told anyone about the hairs on her legs. When she asked, "Yuh understan' wah meh seh?" meaning whether I understood what she said, I made it clear that I did not say anything to anyone. She then tried to scare me by saying that the next day she would be going back to the island of Leguan and I must keep my mouth shut, otherwise she was going to "cut meh rass." After saying that she would spank me if I did not keep it secret, she cuddled me and softly said that she was sorry for striking me yesterday. Seeing a gentle smile on her face, and hearing her say, "Come leh abe mek up," I felt better that she asked to reconcile. I must say that her warm embrace was pleasing, and from that moment our friendship was rekindled.

*****

When I became seven years of age, it was time for me to attend a primary school that was almost half a mile from home. I must say that it was very different from kindergarten, as I now had the responsibility to walk a far distance on my own, and to take care of the new shoes my mother bought me and a slate that I was given to write on.

While returning home from school on the second day, I saw an empty milk can that someone had tossed onto the road. Having seen other boys before walking on a can fastened onto one of their shoes, I wanted to experience it. Without hesitating I stamped on the center of the can with my shoe. Unfortunately, the heel on my shoe came off and immediately I became deeply saddened. Knowing that it was the only pair of shoes I had, I began to worry about how my parents would react when I told them what I did to it. Seeing that there was little I could do about it, I took off my shoes and slowly walked home barefoot.

Later in the evening when my mother returned from work, I nervously told her what had happened. I must say that I was lucky for my mother only cautioned me, saying, "Bai, wha wrang wid yuh head? Yuh see the next time it happen', ah gon wallop yuh batty." Hearing her ask what was wrong with me, and saying that she was going to whip me the next time it happened, I honestly felt I was fortunate not to be spanked. The only thing that still saddened me was that my mother made it clear that for the remaining three days of the week, I would have to go to school barefoot, and wait until the following week for her to buy me another pair of shoes.

It was not long after this incident that I encountered a painful experience that took days to subside. It happened one day while returning from school that I saw a donkey eating grass by the roadside, and decided to tease the animal by pulling its tail. On my first two attempts to pull the donkey's tail, the animal simply moved away from me. Not amused by this, I decided to hold firmly on the donkey's tail, and pull as hard as I could. To my surprise, the animal gave me a fierce kick above my knees, knocking me off my feet before landing on the ground.

Seeing a severe bruise on my left leg, I began to moan with pain. As I sat on the grass weeping, I suddenly heard the voice of someone behind me yelling, "Yuh chupid lil rass! Dah good fu yuh!" Hearing someone telling me that I was stupid and deserved the kick I got, I became reddened with anger. Slowly turning my head, I was surprised to see a man staggering towards me with a bottle in his hand as if he were "tight" (drunk). When this man came close to me and I got the scent of strong liquor some called "sagewan," I shouted at him to go away. Seeing me in a bad mood, he stood quiet for a moment, and then staggered a bit before walking away from me. As soon as he left, I slowly got up and began to walk lamely home. Though it was painful, I managed to limp down the street until I reached home, where my grandmother (ajee) applied some iodine and bandaged my wound.

About a month after this incident, I saw for the first time a man who many felt was mentally unsound because of his unpredictable behavior. I remember returning from school and seeing a group of boys teasing this man by calling him "Walker the nigger." As Walker was taunted, he repeatedly shouted, "British yuh fool!" Though it seemed like fun for these boys who were about a year or two older than me, I was somewhat apprehensive to get close to Walker, who had two large bricks in his hands and was fuming with anger. Suddenly, these boys were taken by surprise when Walker took out a handful of stones that he had hidden under a sheet of newspaper and began to pelt the youths with them. Within seconds, everyone fled the scene except for one boy, who was struck on his leg. As this young boy stood frozen with fear, Walker approached him menacingly and repeatedly said, "British yuh fool!" After intimidating the lad by speaking to him in a harsh tone, an angry Walker marched back to his place in front of a rum shop.

Returning home, I told my grandmother about this incident, and was surprised when she mentioned that Walker came from an educated family, and she knew one of his relatives fairly well. She then cautioned me not to tease or throw stones at Walker because he could seriously hurt me if I made him angry.

Apart from these unforgettable happenings, I must say that between ages seven and eight, I was becoming more observant and this seemed to be a part of growing up. I was very inquisitive and keen to try some of the things that older children did. What fascinated me while attending this primary school was that whenever I visited friends of a higher grade during recess period, my eyes would light up when I saw them using colored crayons to draw pictures of birds and animals on paper. I was also in awe to see children use a fountain pen to draw ink from a small white container that was inserted into a hole on their writing desk.

The only unfortunate thing about attending this primary school was being bullied on a number of occasions by boys who liked to pick on those that were small. It was not until I had gathered enough courage, almost a year later, to tell my father about being bullied that he decided to send me to another school.

*****

When I became nine years of age, I was happy to be given a brand-new school bag along with a set of books and pencils, and to attend a new school that was recently built in our area. Unfortunately, on the first day of school, I received two lashes on my buttocks from the principal for standing in the wrong line to get enrolled into my class. I must say that some of the teachers of this school were quick to punish anyone, even for a minor mistake. I clearly remember being spanked at school for being late and also for keeping my fingernails dirty. The reason for not being on time was that twice a week I had to fetch water, as well as to clean the "draina" (gutter) in our yard and to feed the chickens before going to school.

One day while returning from school, I became overwhelmed with joy when I found a twenty-five-cent coin on the road. As I held the money and looked at it pryingly, it appeared dull and partly rusted. Excited by what I had found, I hurriedly took off one of my shoes, and then picked up a wet piece of mud from the ground to clean the coin. After putting mud onto the coin, I used the heel of my foot to polish the money on both sides. After this, I washed it with some water from a nearby stream, and was pleased to see how clean it became. I then hurriedly put my shoe back on, and while holding the coin firmly in my hand, I began to think about the number of tasty things I could buy with it. Not wanting anyone to see the coin, it dawned on me to purchase something to eat so as to change the money.

Arriving at the first shop I saw, I bought a small bottle of lemonade for three cents and the end part of a cake called "coconut roll" for one cent. I was very nervous when approaching the shopkeeper, fearing that if he questioned me about where I got the money, I might not know what to say to him. Fortunately, I was not questioned, and after eating hurriedly, I went to another shop further down the road to spend some more of the money. With twenty-one cents remaining, I decided to buy an ice cream cone for five cents and a large sweet that was the size of a golf ball, called "never-done," for the price of one cent. By this time my tummy was full and felt like a rock. Minutes later, I felt as though I had gotten what many locals call "Niggaritis," a condition of being so uncomfortable from overeating that you started to feel sluggish. Shortly after, I developed a pain in my tummy, and was gently rubbing it, when a man riding a bicycle made fun of me by saying, "Wha happen bai? Yuh walkin' like ah tight shit brace yuh!" With his remark that I was walking as though I wanted to go badly to the toilet, I felt uneasy that I could not let anyone know that the problem I was experiencing was a result of eating too much.

As I got closer to home, I began to think about what to do with the remaining change I had. The most money I ever got from anyone was a penny, and if my parents were to find out that I had fifteen cents, they would definitely accuse me of stealing from someone. After pondering for a while, I decided to throw the remaining change into a trench that was about thirty yards away from home. Though it grieved me to toss away that amount of money, I felt that I had to get rid of it, fearing I might be accused of theft.

Apart from these experiences, which became etched in my mind over the years, I continued to enjoy life. With so many of my cousins and friends attending the same school as me, I never got bored. Though I was from a poor family, there was plenty for me to eat, as in practically every yard in our neighborhood there were lots of trees to pick fruits from such as mangoes, bananas, guavas, coconuts, papayas, gooseberries, etc. At times when I did not feel like having fruit, I would go to the chicken pens in our yard to pick up an egg, which I would then ask my grandmother to cook for me. I recall on some occasions going to the chicken pens and seeing a hen in the midst of laying an egg. Being afraid that the egg would become cracked if it were to hit the floor of the pen, I would catch the egg with my hands before it fell.

An incident that occasionally brings back memories of the past happened while climbing a tree one day to pick some small, purplish-black fruits called "jamoons." As I leaned on a limb of the tree to pick the fruit, I was taken by surprise to see a little bird in a nest. As I cautiously moved between the branches to get closer to it, the young bird, in attempting to fly away, tumbled between the branches and fell to the ground. Seconds later, I heard the bird chirping and in a jiffy, I climbed down the tree to pick it up. But from nowhere a yellow-breasted bird with brown upper parts, popularly known as a "kiskadee," appeared and began to hover closely over my head. Being afraid of this aggressive bird, I hurriedly ran home with the fledgling.

With a strong desire to keep the young bird as a pet, I carefully put it into an empty shoebox. Thinking that it might be hungry, I ran down the alley with the bird in the open box to pick a ripe mango from a tree. I then took a "chinkee" (tiny) piece of the mango and brought it close to the little bird's beak. But instead of eating, it began to chirp in a distressing manner. As I stood puzzled, the "kiskadee" suddenly appeared and began to peck me on the head. In spite of being attacked, I was determined not to release the young bird, so I hastily ran into our house with it. However, when my grandmother heard it chirping, she came out of her room asking where I got the bird from. In an angry tone she said, "Bai wha wrang wid yuh? Yuh prappa bad! Nah mek me an' yuh fall out!" When she said that I was very bad, and not to make us fall out, I began to explain how I got the bird. However, she appeared displeased and tried to scare me by saying that the "kiskadee" was the parent of the young bird, and as long as I kept the little bird; its mother would keep following me to "jook" (pierce) my eyes with its beak. What she said was not enough to deter me from keeping the little bird. It was not until she asked how my mother would feel if someone were to take me away from her that I had a change of heart. Becoming somewhat sympathetic, I decided to take the little bird back to the nest where I found it.

At the break of dawn on most days, it was a joy for me to walk beneath a huge "sapodilla" tree and the "golden apple" tree in our yard to pick up the ripe fruits that had fallen on the ground. Though many of the fruits were partly eaten by birds, that did not stop me from cutting off what was bad, before feasting on the rest of the fruit. After eating, it was habitual for me to sit on a bench in our yard and to watch a variety of birds fly from one tree to the next. It was awesome to watch hummingbirds move swiftly through the air and vanish quickly from my sight. Then from nowhere this little bird would suddenly appear again, hovering over plants, leaving me wondering how it was possible for me to catch a bird with such speed. To hear other birds, such as a "blue-saki" making a chirping sound, or parrots making excited tones, sometimes led me to believe that these birds wanted to attract others.

Sitting and waiting patiently for other birds to appear often got me into trouble, especially when my grandmother yelled from her window, "Bai, ah wah yuh ah do?" With her asking what I was doing, I could sense that at any moment she was going to shout at me to stop staring at the birds and to get ready for school. At times when I ran about in the yard chasing butterflies early in the mornings, I clearly remember, my grandmother would say, "Yuh hard ears! Stop galavantin' befuh ah tell yuh fadda!" With her telling me that I was stubborn and for me to stop wasting time before she complained to my father, it was common for me to say to her, "Ah comin' jus' now!"

It angered me at times while birdwatching when a stray cat suddenly appeared and tried to catch a little "god-bird" while it searched for food among the fallen leaves in our garden. Also, I could not help getting angry at the sight of a hawk lurking high in the air, only to witness how quickly all the birds would disappear when they sensed danger. All in all, it was a treat to the eyes to watch various birds, insects, reptiles, and even small monkeys, commonly called "saki-winki." I must say that the large number of fruit trees and plants in our yard, and those of our neighbors, certainly attracted lots of birds and animals.

Apart from these challenging experiences, there was one particular incident at age nine that became engraved in my mind. This happened when a few friends and I had seen for the first time a man who assumed the dress and manner of a woman. While playing in an open area near a bus stop, we were taken aback to see this man with make-up on his face, and strutting around with a lady's handbag.

Being uncertain about this oddly dressed person, my friends and I were apprehensive about getting close to him, fearing he might get angry and chase us away.

After the stranger waited at the bus stop for about twenty minutes without the bus coming, we were taken by surprise when he quickly ran and jumped onto the back of a cart that was drawn by a horse as it passed by. It seemed that he got frustrated waiting for a bus and decided to steal a ride on a horse cart. When the driver of the cart looked around and saw him, he repeatedly shouted, "Get aff! Get aff! Yuh chupid antiman!" After hollering at the man to get off, and calling him a homosexual, the driver brought his cart to a halt. Within seconds, the strangely dressed man came off the cart and began to quarrel with the driver for calling him an "antiman." As they traded harsh words, I remembered the man saying to the driver of the cart, "Wha wrang wid yuh, eh? Leh meh tell yuh somethin'! Ah wud scratch yuh! Ah wud bite yuh! Ah wud bruk yuh rass!" While this man threatened to scratch and bite the driver, we were left in shock when the horse suddenly became excited by a mare about a hundred yards away and began to gallop after her with the cart. I must say that this serious incident suddenly turned hilarious, as it was fun to laugh our heads off at the driver of the cart, running down the road to stop his stallion from chasing the mare.

*****

On the weekends it was common to see a number of boys playing or swimming in shallow trenches, and catching schools of a small fish many called "cacabelly." I recall one day, while sitting on a bridge with three friends, dangling our legs over a shallow stream, I encouraged them to follow me to a dumpsite to fetch the top of an old car. After telling them we could have lots of fun if we put it into a trench about three feet deep and used it as a boat, they were delighted with my idea.

A while later when we turned the "car top" onto its smooth side and put it into the water, I quickly sat in it before the rest of my friends got a chance to do so. I was so thrilled that I began to sing "Michael Row the Boat Ashore, Hallelujah!" I must admit that while singing and pretending to be sailing in a boat down a river, the other boys toiled in the water to push it along.

After a while my friends who were doing the pushing began to quarrel among themselves, as each of them felt it was their turn next to sit in the improvised boat. Sadly, our fun quickly ended when all three of them decided to climb into the boat with me, causing it to sink quickly to the bottom of the water.

Playing in these trenches was not entirely safe because some of us occasionally got a serious cut or bruise on our feet from a broken bottle or the waste that some people threw into the trenches. I remember once getting a severe cut above my ankle. Taking the advice of some boys, I took some of the soft mud from the trench and placed it over the cut to prevent it from bleeding. With mud on my wound, I sat patiently in the sun waiting for it to dry on the cut, not thinking about the danger of something that could turn out to be extremely harmful. I can only say that many of us survived serious infection because of our strong immune system. Aside from this, many of us, while walking through swamps and trenches, occasionally had to remove bloodsucking leeches that clung onto our legs, or we might discover days later that we got a fungal infection from ringworm.

Later that day when I returned home and was questioned by my parents, my excuse for being too long away from home was that I went to play a game of cricket with friends. Seconds later, I realized I was in trouble when my father looked at me in the face and yelled, "Don't lie to meh! Yuh went swimmin'! Look at yuh face, it gat crapo-beard pon it!" The "crapo-beard" he was referring to was short, hair-like dirt that sometimes appeared around your mouth when swimming or playing in trenches.

After uttering those strong words, my father gave me a stern look when he gazed at the cut on my foot. Furious, he said, "Bai, wha di rass yuh do to yuh foot?" After he asked what I did to my foot, I gave him a sad look as if I were about to cry. I must say that in spite of my trying to get some sympathy, my father gave me a few lashes before yelling, "Go bade yuh skin!" With him ordering me to take a shower, I immediately did what I was told. He then treated my wound with iodine and bandaged the cut.

Over the years it was common for many young boys to get spanked when they spent too much time away from home. With many of us time and again hearing our parents use harsh words such as, "Yuh wutliss! Yuh dotish! Yuh hard ears! Ah gon box yuh! Ah gon cut yuh tail!," some of us could sense when we were going to get spanked for doing something our parents felt was seriously wrong.

At age nine, I must say that some children my age were not afraid to walk long distances by themselves, because a child being kidnapped or killed was practically unheard of. I remember walking almost a mile by myself to catch crabs along the seashore. The only fear I had was pushing my hand in a hole and getting a snap on my fingers by a crab's "tengle-leh" (claw). I even recall walking by the "seawall" that was built along the foreshore with young friends to fly kites at Easter, and no one would harm us. As an example of how strict the laws were, I once overheard my grandfather and his fellow retired detectives discussing how they had given six lashes to a man just before he was put into a prison cell for stealing more than once, and how they gave him six lashes on the day he was released from prison, so as to remind him not to steal again. The term they used in those days was "Six in and six out."

In addition to my fond memories of playing in trenches, what has also remained unforgettable from age nine was that at least three times a year my cousins and I were given a laxative of either castor oil or senna pods by our parents. As young children we hated the taste of these medicines, which our parents claimed would give us "belly wok" (diarrhea) so as to purge our system.

*****

Age ten was the most challenging period of my life, and I recall taking a number of serious risks in which I could easily have been killed. Seeing what other boys had done, I took a chance once in a while, to place a large nail on one of the lines of a train track so that the train would run over it to make a chisel-like tool. Using the flattened nail, I would then carve out my own toy gun from a piece of wood.

I remember on a few occasions how the driver of the train would honk its horn for me to move. But being determined, I would lie on the ground, holding the nail on the line until the train was about thirty yards away before letting go and quickly rolling away from the tracks. The reason for holding the nail as long as possible was to prevent it from rolling off the line because of the vibration on the train tracks.

In those days when trains were a popular means of transportation, now and again my friends and I would climb onto the last two carriages of a train when it stopped to pick up passengers, so as to get a handful of molasses that overflowed onto the sides of huge containers. I must admit that my parents were totally unaware about the risk I took getting so close to the wheels of a train. What eventually put an end to this terrible habit of mine was the death of a cow when it tried to cross the railway tracks as a train was approaching. To see the animal get "lick dong" (hit) and its body torn apart left me in dismay, realizing that the same could happen to me if I were to get hit by a train.

Another incident that brings back memories of the past happened while I was passing an old, empty, rundown house with a few friends, when one of them began encouraging the rest of us to pelt the house with stones. We were told that the house had a "backoo," a spirit of short stature, living in it.

While stoning the house, my uncle, who happened to be passing by on a bicycle, saw me among the boys and yelled, "Bai, yuh head good or yuh gaan mad? Come hay, right now!" With him asking me if I were crazy and to come to him immediately, I had no choice but to obey him. Unfortunately, as soon as I got close to him, he took off his belt and smacked me twice on my buttocks before ordering me to go home immediately.

Later, when it became nighttime, I approached my grandmother before going to sleep, asking her to tell me a few bedtime stories. My grandmother was a good storyteller, and with a solemn look, she told me tales called "Jumbee" stories that were about evil beings. These tales about spirits that could frighten or harm me were very scary. However, in spite of being apprehensive about these intriguing stories, I still wanted to hear them.

After a few nights of listening to my grandmother's tales, I could not sleep, especially when pondering on stories about a woman called an "Ol' Higue" who sucked the blood of children when they were sound asleep. What scared me the most was the story of a very tall man called a "Moon-gazer," who stood on the road with his legs apart, and if children were to walk between his legs, he would bring them together to crush them. Even though I lay between my sister and a brother in the same bed, I was afraid that demons would come out at night to harm me. Now and again when I woke up my parents to tell them that I was afraid of the dark, they often yelled at me not to disturb them.

One night as my father lay sound asleep after a hard day's work, I woke him up suddenly to tell him that I saw a demon. Fuming with anger he yelled, "Come hay bai! Come fuh some licks!" With him ordering me to come to him for a spanking, I kept at a distance and began to rub my eyes so as not to make eye contact with him. However, this poor attempt to get sympathy did not deter him from smacking me a few times on my buttocks, before cautioning me never to mention anything about demons. I must say that from that day onward I was no longer afraid of the dark, fearing that if I ever woke my father to tell him about demons, I would be spanked. Early the next morning, my father angrily marched into his mother's room and told her not to tell me any more scary stories.

Days later, I received another spanking. However, on this occasion I had done something seriously wrong that greatly annoyed my father. I was caught trying to smoke a cigarette butt that someone had thrown away. I must say that after the spanking I received, I never touched a cigarette to this day. I even remember my father's words, "Yuh lil rass! Yuh wan' play big man, eh? Ah gon cut yuh tail wid dis tamarind whip!" To hear him demand if I wanted to act like an adult, and that he was going to whip my butt, drew me to understand that he was totally against young people smoking.

After these happenings, I began to ponder more on the consequences of my actions before doing something that I honestly felt was wrong. To keep me occupied after school, my father gave me the additional chore of taking a couple of his sheep to areas that had lush grass for them to eat. I must say that this particular chore significantly reduced my playing time with friends in the evenings.

*****

A few months later, while attempting to catch a small school of fish that were under a bridge, my eyes lit up when I saw a snake in the water. Having no fear at the moment, I quickly ran to get a stick about five feet long to attack the snake. As I approached it, I remembered an earlier incident when some friends and I had tried to kill a young "camoudi" (boa constrictor) in water and had failed to do. Believing that it would be easier to kill a snake on land than in water, I quickly put the end of the stick underneath the snake and hoisted it onto dry land. Immediately, I charged at the serpent to hit it, but each time I tried to strike the snake, it kept moving quickly away. Suddenly, I was taken aback when the serpent stood up practically on its tail, in a position to attack me. My heart started to race for it was the first time I saw a snake react in this manner. However, I was determined to kill it, and after giving it a series of blows, the snake eventually lay still and died.

I then headed back towards the bridge that was across the stream. But this time I was more cautious, and before going under the bridge to catch the fish, I carefully looked around to ensure there were no snakes. On this occasion I had a pleasant surprise, as in a far corner below the bridge I saw a dozen duck eggs in an unattended nest. Excited, I immediately ran home and told my father what I saw. He then gave me a saucepan with a piece of cloth inside and told me to bring the eggs home.

Coming back for the eggs, I saw a close friend of mine nicknamed Blackie coming to meet me. At the time, he was sucking a sweet, reddish cube of ice called "flutie." But as soon as Blackie cast eyes on me, he yelled "no stings!" meaning that he would not share what he was eating. The term "yuh go in fuh stings" was a verbal agreement between young friends that if someone wanted to have a piece of what you were eating, he or she had to quickly yell "stings!" With my thoughts fixed on the eggs, I distracted

Blackie by telling him that I was taking the saucepan to an aunt a few streets away. Blackie, who was of East Indian descent and dark in complexion, was one of my closest friends who came almost every day to play with me. On this occasion, I urged him to go in the meantime to my neighbor's yard where some of our friends were eating sugar cane. I had to lie to him, for if he saw the eggs, he would definitely want half of them.

Returning home with the eggs, my father placed all of them under a fowl hen that was sitting on a couple of her own eggs at the time. I was somewhat puzzled when he took the hen's two eggs from under her and brought them close to his ear. After shaking each egg, he said to me that they were both "ganda eggs" (spoilt eggs) and that I should throw them away in a nearby trench. Shortly after, I became happy when I saw the hen use her beak to move the duck eggs under her body. Witnessing how she slowly wiggled her body to cover the eggs, I was pleased that she had accepted them as her own.

Weeks later when the eggs began to hatch, I sat for almost an hour one Sunday morning to see now and again a new duckling push its head out from under the hen. Later in the day, something strange happened when two ducklings came out, and step-by-step they walked about a foot away from the hen. Immediately, I became excited and quickly picked them up with both hands. However, while I was admiring them, they suddenly jumped out of my hands and ran under the hen. Seeing me puzzled, my grandmother, who was quietly observing what I was doing, shouted from her window, "Yuh know why de ducklings get away unda de fowl?" As I stood bewildered when she asked me if I knew why the ducklings ran under the hen, she told me to look up at the huge "golden apple" tree in our yard. I was in shock when I saw a hawk looking keenly at the hen. My grandmother then advised me to scare the hawk away before it flew down and scooped up one of the ducklings. In a flash, I picked up a stone and threw it at the hawk, and immediately it spread its wings and quickly flew away.

Taking care of these ducklings gave me a sense of responsibility, and in the months to follow it was a joy to watch them grow. Seeing how attentive I was to these birds, my father sensed that I was maturing in age. I was given more responsible chores such as purchasing stamps from the local post office, and going once a week to buy food items from a nearby grocery store. I must say that I really enjoyed going to the post office, as it was an opportunity for me to talk to the well-dressed postmen who were very polite.

The most memorable task I was given at age ten happened one night when my father gave me an empty rice bag and told me to follow him to the animal pen in our yard, where a cat had her litter of seven kittens. He said that no one wanted these kittens and he had to get rid of them. I was told to open the bag, and in a jiffy he put all the kittens into the bag and quickly tied the mouth of it. He then said to me to take the kittens to a nearby church and to release them next to a garbage bin. My father felt that with the excess food that was thrown away at times by church members, these kittens would not go hungry.

Arriving at the church, I discovered that it was filled with people. Eagerly looking around, I could not see the garbage bin my father had mentioned except for a small one that was close to the main entrance of the temple. Feeling a bit nervous about what I was sent to do, and thinking that the small garbage bin at the entrance was probably the one my father mentioned, I quickly untied the bag and released the kittens. But the moment I did that, they all ran into the church, causing some women and children to scream, as the young cats ran wildly between them. Afraid about what I did, I ran home as fast as I could. When my father saw me return home with the empty bag, he assumed everything went well.

Days after this incident, my good friend Blackie introduced me to one of his friends, whom he nicknamed Bruk-Up. I felt sympathetic when I discovered that he was a polio victim. It touched me to see him with a pleasant smile on his face while limping on one leg that had a brace support.

Becoming more and more acquainted with Bruk-Up as the days went by, I discovered he was a well-mannered lad with an amicable disposition. He was not the type who would tease anyone, get into mischief or cheat others in friendly games.

It took months after I was introduced to Bruk-Up to see him get angry for the first time. This happened one evening when Blackie and I saw Bruk-Up at a nearby shop, having a glass of a local drink called "mauby" and eating a small loaf of bread, that cost a "jill" (penny), with cheese. Upon seeing Bruk-Up, Blackie shouted, "Oh rass banna! Wha happenin' dey?" After greeting Bruk-Up, a curious Blackie decided to ask him where he got money to buy the food he was eating. When Bruk-Up replied that he got money from selling empty bottles, Blackie replied, "Yuh makin' joke!", meaning he was not serious. As Bruk-Up ignored him and continued eating, I could not believe that Blackie had the nerve to ask him for a piece of his bread with cheese. Knowing that only an hour ago Blackie and I had sat in a tree and ate about a dozen guavas, I felt it was unfair to ask Bruk-Up to share his food, because he was not able like us to climb trees and pick fruits. What drew me to think that Bruk-Up was a special friend was how willingly he broke off a piece of his bread to give Blackie. Unfortunately, this kind deed turned sour when Blackie refused what he was offered, claiming that he did not want to eat from the part of the bread that Bruk-Up had put his mouth on; instead, he wanted a piece from the other end that was not touched. Deeply annoyed,

Bruk-Up yelled, "Yuh like fuh play bigass wid yuhself! Yuh gat tu much style! Tek it or lef it, eh?" With him commenting on Blackie's attitude and demanding that he either take it or leave it, Blackie was in shock by his sudden outburst. Bruk-Up furiously added, "Ah gon teach yuh tail ah lesson!" In a jiffy, Bruk-Up stuffed the entire remaining portion of the bread he had into his mouth, leaving Blackie in total disbelief. Though minor disputes like this sometimes brought harsh words, most of us were quick to reconcile and put aside our differences so as not to end our friendship.

*****

Growing up in Guyana was not only exciting for young boys, for girls had lots to laugh at and to smile about. Some of them not only played cricket, they also climbed fruit trees and even played among boys using "awara" (fruit) seeds as marbles. At times when young girls were caught climbing trees, some boys would tease them by telling them that the fruit on the tree would become sour. I recall a girl being repeatedly teased by a boy, and in anger she yelled, "Yuh manish! Move yuh tail from hay befuh ah kick-yuh-up!" After harshly telling him that he was bad and to go away before she beat him, the boy immediately stopped teasing her.

Occasionally, it was fun for us boys to join a group of girls playing a game called "hopscotch." An incident I recall while playing with girls was being hit on my head by a girl nicknamed Smiley. While hopping on one leg in a few circles and squares, I was accused of letting my foot touch the edge of one of the squares. In disputing her claim, both of us got very angry and began to quarrel. Annoyed with her telling me that I was a barefaced liar, I told her that her teeth were bigger than her mouth. When I began to giggle about it, Smiley pointed her finger in my face and yelled, "Yuh playin'wrang an' strang! Stop skinnin' yuh teeth!" After telling me I was wrong and that I was pretending not to be at fault, Smiley yelled at me to stop jeering. Filled with rage, she picked up a dry coconut branch that was sometimes used as a cricket bat and hit me "whaddax whaddax" on my head.

Our dispute that day did not sour our friendship for long, as on the following day, Smiley came by our house to play with my sister. When Smiley mentioned to my sister how rude I was to her, my sister insisted that I apologize to her. Knowing that Smiley was her closest friend, I lowered my head and said I was sorry. But this was not pleasing to Smiley, for she vehemently said that I would not be allowed to play with her friends unless I looked at her in the face to apologize. Not wanting to be left out or to miss any fun, I slowly lifted up my head to make an apology. By the end of the day, Smiley and I became the best of friends. Things got even better when my friend Blackie and I joined Smiley and her friends to play a number of games such as "drop it Peter boy," "one, two, three, red light!," "dog and de bone," "ketcha," and a game called "littie," using five small stones.

In the village where I lived, it was common in the evenings to see young girls being taken by their teenage sisters or relatives for leisurely walks. Watching many of them nicely dressed with a colorful ribbon in their hair, and occasionally holding each other's hands in a protective manner when a car passed by, often reminded me that I had to be careful when crossing busy roads.

To scare some of these girls who were returning home at nightfall, my friends and I would tie a bicycle tube with a piece of string, and slowly pull it across the road so as to frighten them into believing that it was a snake. But when we were caught hiding in a cluster of bush, giggling at them, some of these angry girls would pelt us with stones.

At times it was amusing to see some girls scare away a stray dog, often called a "rice-eater," that was barking or coming to attack them. It was somewhat amusing, when some girls pretended that they were picking up stones to throw at a dog, to see the animal put its tail between its legs and run away. I could only guess that with stray dogs being stoned now and again by boys, the animal sensed that the moment someone leaned one hand to the ground, they were going to throw stones at them.

On some occasions, teasing girls could be troubling for us boys. I recall once teasing a young girl who had on a frilly, pink dress, telling her that she looked like a "stargyal." Though I complimented her about looking like an actress, she got furious and "stew she teeth" at me, making a hissing sound of disapproval. Not happy with what I had said, she yelled, "Yuh playin' fresh wid yuhself! Yuh like ah force ripe mango!" When she somewhat implied that I was "hitting" on her and trying to act like an adult, I told her, after she "stew she teeth" a second time, not to kiss me from so far away, but to come closer. Furious, she hastily went home and told her eldest sister, who shortly after came storming down the road towards me with an umbrella in her hand. The moment this big girl got near me, she pointed her umbrella in my face and yelled, "Yuh tek yuh eyes pass meh lil sista, eh? Don't tease she again!" After saying that I had no respect for her sister, she hit me on the head with her umbrella and angrily walked away. I must say that many older girls were very protective of their younger sisters and would even walk right up to a group of boys and caution them not to be disrespectful.

As young children, the vast majority of us never harbored ill feelings for one another for long periods, because most of us were quick to put aside our differences so as to enjoy the fun of playing together. An interesting thing to note is that many children, regardless of whether they came from the countryside or Georgetown, had a nickname such as Fat Bai, Baby Girl, Galo, Girley, Fine Bai, Buck, Tarzan, Barney, Chinee, etc. It is interesting that the majority accepted the false name someone gave them, and even as adults they were still called by their nickname.

Months later, it became a joyous occasion when my grandmother asked me to go to a nearby Hindu temple to give a message to an elderly man named Makhan, that she wanted to see him. When meeting this gentleman, who at the time was wearing khaki clothing, I recalled that he could not communicate well in English. I actually had to point to our house and signal to him to follow me, before he understood what I was trying to say. I must say that he was a humble man, for he willingly trailed behind me to our house.

Upon seeing my grandmother, Makhan immediately began to communicate with her in the Hindi language. Minutes later, my grandmother gave him a bowl of dyed rice. After Makhan left, I questioned my grandmother about the reason for giving him the raw rice. She then gave me the good news that one of my father's brothers would be getting married, and Makhan would be giving small amounts of the dyed rice to many of our relatives and neighbors in the area, as an invitation to attend the wedding.

About six weeks later, preparations for the wedding began and a huge tent was set up in our backyard. I was surprised to see the large quantities of rice, flour, pumpkin, split peas and potatoes that were brought to our house by relatives. Utensils such as cooking pots, bowls, buckets, etc. were borrowed from a nearby Hindu temple. I must add that on the night before the wedding a number of men and women, mostly distant relatives, arrived to assist in the preparation of food for the following day.

Finally, on the day of the marriage ceremony, I was in awe to see the large number of people who came to attend it. The celebrations for this wedding lasted for seven straight days, and it was pleasing to see that even people who weren't invited were welcomed to eat and enjoy themselves. It was fun for us children to watch a number of men and women dance to the rhythms of "tassa drums" and to the lively tunes of a jukebox.

*****

At age eleven, my mother bought me a light soccer ball that I had always wanted. One day while playing with it a fair distance from home, I was approached by a group of boys about my age, demanding that I give them my ball or they would cuff me. Just as they were about to pounce on me, a tall, strong boy yelled at them to leave me alone, otherwise he was going to beat them. Seeing this muscular boy, whom I later nicknamed Dougla because he was of a mixed race, they immediately refrained from hitting me and furiously walked away. After this incident, a warm friendship developed between Dougla and me. We became such close friends that practically every day, Dougla would bring a few of his friends for us to play a game of cricket.

About three weeks later, my aunt from England sent me an expensive toy called Viewmaster as a gift. I was overjoyed when I got this camera-like device, which carried a rotary disk that had some of the most beautiful scenes of places in Europe. The first person I allowed to see my Viewmaster was my best friend Dougla. It did not take long for other boys in our neighborhood to learn that I had this expensive toy. However, when they surrounded me one day, asking me to show it to them, I demanded that they pay me one cent. When four boys took out their money to pay me, I told them to give it to Dougla, so that they would not gang up on me later and take away the money they paid.

For those boys who had no money and wished to see

my pictures, I encouraged them to "scale de palin"(jump over the fence) to steal fruits from their neighbor's yard and bring them to me. As more and more boys pleaded with their parents for a "frek" (money), Dougla and I benefited, as we were able to buy cakes and the local drink "mauby." With Dougla being a loyal friend who was usually there to protect me, my confidence quickly grew, for I was no longer timid. My deportment changed, for whenever some boys brought me fruits that were partly rotten, I would insult them. Feeling like a leader among other boys, I realized that even my strong friend Dougla was obedient when I demanded that I got to bat first whenever we played cricket. It seemed that with him frequently getting a penny from me, as well as fruits to eat, he tried not to say anything to offend me.

One day while I was at school, I was told by my teacher that all the children in our class and some from a higher grade had to go to a distant playing field because the Prime Minister of our country would be passing by, and we had to wave at him. After waiting about two hours on a hot sunny day, I saw the Prime Minister on a horse, along with a tall, tough-looking man who was his bodyguard. Suddenly it dawned on me that he was no different from me, as he too needed someone to protect him. Thinking about my loyal friend Dougla, I came to think that our Prime Minister would be old one day, and it was possible that when I grew up, I could become the leader of Guyana with Dougla as my bodyguard. These wishful thoughts never came to fruition, as I was taken by surprise a few weeks later when Dougla informed me that he and his parents would be moving to another village to live. This was a huge concern for me, as I quickly realized that I could no longer be rude to boys in our area, fearing that when Dougla left, they might seek revenge and beat me. Such fears brought about a change in my deportment, as I became friendlier with those I used to be rude to.

With time I started to think and act more maturely. This came about when I began to listen to adults talk about politics, which was a hot topic at the time. I also began to listen to the BBC news and to the simple sayings and meaningful stories my grandparents taught me.

My grandfather was a passionate sports fan who loved boxing, and whenever fights were broadcast over the radio, he would encourage me to listen. I could never forget that day when he invited a few of his friends to listen to a world title fight between Muhammad Ali (then called Cassius Clay) and Sonny Liston. I remember that during the fight his old tube radio would suddenly stop playing, but whenever this happened, he would hit the sides of the radio to get it to play again. At times I was in awe to see that when he struck the radio, tiny round particles of dust, which some called "granny sugar," came out of it. These falling particles made my grandmother a little angry, for after the fight, she would tell my grandfather to clean the "dutty" (dirt) on the floor.

Aside from this, the radio my grandfather owned was shared by many of our family members. I remember from a tender age listening to one of my aunts, who amid preparing breakfast, hummed her favorite Indian songs as they played on the radio. At nights it was common to see some of my uncles in a joyful mood when listening to songs by calypsonians such as Lord Kitchener, King Fighter and Mighty Sparrow. To my uncles, some of the songs that were sung by these singers were full of life, as the lyrics conveyed an amusing story that gave them a great deal to smile about. On other occasions, I heard them burst into laughter when listening to comedians such as Sam Chase and Jack Melo on the radio.

Later in the night when it was my grandmother's turn to listen to the radio, everyone was usually asked to be quiet, because she wanted to listen to a radio program called Death Announcements. In our house, this was the last program that most of us listened to before going to bed. From time to time many of us were astonished when my grandmother, listening to the announcements, would say that one of our relatives had passed away. With a look of concern, she would then explain to the adults how they were related to the person who died, and how important it was for them to attend the funeral. Though the radio program was a sad one, it often reminded many of us about the fragility of life, and the need for us to support those in mourning. I remember my grandmother telling my aunts and uncles that they should always keep in contact with their relatives and friends. It was her wish that all of us live in harmony with our relations, and not become a selfish generation that cared only about ourselves.

*****

Growing up with friends of different races such as Portuguese, Chinese, and Afro-Guyanese, I must say that as young boys we had close friendships. Though many of us belonged to different faiths, we were very open-minded and lived for the greater part in harmony. I recall at the end of Ramadan going to a mosque with young boys about my age to partake in the food that was shared. On the Hindu celebration of Phagwah, it was pleasing to see the number of Christian and Muslim children who enjoyed taking part in this spring festival.

Christmas was a time of giving, and it was fun for young boys and girls to show one another the toys they got. Though many of us did not get gifts from our parents, we were happy to make our own toys such as sling shots, toy guns, buck-tops, and even rubber balls made by wrapping slices of a bicycle tube around "awara" seeds. Some who were a couple of years older than me were not only good at making scooters and go-carts, but also showed maturity when assisting their parents on Saturdays to sell fruits and vegetables at a local marketplace. I must add that some boys were well-rounded for, amid all their fun in play, it was pleasing to their loved ones that they had passed the Common Entrance Examination, and were able to attend some of the best schools in the country.

Aside from this it was challenging once in a while for younger boys to catch an insect commonly called a "marabunta," and to put it into an empty matchbox with a small hole on one side. Then, with the insect moving around inside the box and making a buzzing sound, you could imagine listening to a radio. I must say that it was risky to catch a "marabunta" by throwing a handful of wet mud onto a nest, as some of these insects could dart out of it to inflict a sting that could be painful and irritating.

One of my favorite toys that I learned to make from a tender age required an empty wooden thread reel, a piece of candle wax, a rubber band, and a matchstick to make a toy that could climb over small objects. A plaything that was popular among boys but not too pleasing to some adults was the "carbon bomb." Using an empty Ovaltine can, you would put a piece of carbon in it, spit in the can and shake it. After this, you put a lighted match to a hole at the bottom of the can, and a loud boom was heard as the cover got blown off.

For many of us the game called "cowboys and Indians" gave us a lot to laugh and to smile about. Using rubber bands made from slices of a bicycle tube to launch small seeds called "buck beads" as tiny missiles, at times we ran amid "plimpla" (thorny) bushes or between neighboring houses to attack or to escape from one another.

At Christmas it was a special treat to see children from different areas following a "Mother Sally" masquerade band, that had a tall image of a woman being accompanied by colorfully dressed musicians. It was a joy to see the place bustling with activity on Christmas and Boxing Day. While many celebrated Christmas Day at home with their relatives and friends, it was common for some men to celebrate the festive occasion with friends in nearby rum shops.

I recollect, on Christmas Eve one year, seeing a drunk man carrying a roll of linoleum floor covering on his shoulder and singing the song, "Drink ah rum on ah Christmas mornin', drink ah rum, Mamma drink if yuh drinkin." While he sang his heart out, I was amused to see his wife storming down the road and yelling at him to bring the linoleum home, as she wanted to "put away de house" (spruce up their home) before Christmas Day.

During the festive season, it was wonderful to listen to people talk about the various foods they were preparing for their families and invited guests. Listening to people talk about food sometimes made your "mouth leh-leh" (drool) when they mentioned garlic pork, salt beef, peppa-pot, roast pork, baked turkey, fowl curry, duck curry, etc. It was also a special treat to enjoy the rich taste of homemade ice cream, black cake, sorrel drink and ginger beer.

An interesting note about festive occasions is that even though most of us belonged to different faiths, becoming a Hindu, a Muslim or a Christian for one day showed how open-minded many young children were. I always remember, growing up in Guyana, seeing my grandmother, who was a devout Hindu, praying in her room. Even though she was a Hindu, I could not comprehend what faith she really belonged to, for among the Hindu deities she had in her room, there were also statues of Jesus and Mother Mary.

*****

The game of cricket was the favorite hobby of most boys in our area, for practically every day after school many of us would either meet in parks, in a neighbor's yard, or even to play on the public roads. Many of us liked the game so much that we would even play cricket in the pouring rain. After a game in the rain, a few of us, when the sun eventually appeared, would sit on the ground in the open pasture and allow ourselves to get dry. Other boys who were not fond of doing so would return home after play, and take a "sponge down" (brief clean up) from a vat or pipe in their yard.

I recall one day, while playing cricket on a road where cars occasionally passed, two policemen in a vehicle called the "Bongo Van" suddenly appeared to arrest us. As they hastily got out of their van, a few boys managed to run away; however, four us did not get a chance to escape. We were then hurried into the police vehicle where they began to terrorize us about putting us in prison if we did not stop playing cricket on the public roads. In those days policemen did not charge anyone our age for playing in restricted areas; however, to deter us from doing so, some of them would give us a slap or two on the face.

A few months after this incident, my mother gave short notice when she informed me that she would be taking me to the island of Leguan where I was born to see my relatives who lived there. I was very excited when she said this, as it was a different part of the country where I rarely get the opportunity to go.

On the morning of our departure, my mother give me a fresh bath using a non-perfumed soap that was mainly used for washing clothes and dishes, called "salt soap." She then dressed me in fresh clothing, and rubbed a fair amount of Vaseline on my hair to make me look well-groomed. I must say that it greatly annoyed me when my mother "rumfled up" my hair with the greasy gel before combing it. Amid it all I was pleased when she said, "Come bai! Leh meh put on ah buckta pon yuh." It was the first time in my life that I put on a boy's underwear, and I became so excited that I ran into the living room to show my grandmother.

After my mother dressed me with my shirt neatly tucked into my pants, my grandmother cheerfully said with a broad smile on her face, "Yuh look like ah real edger boy in yuh new dan-dan." She was hinting that I looked sharply dressed in my new clothes. While my mother and my grandmother fussed over me, I felt somewhat uncomfortable in the clothing I had on, as it irritated my skin. It seemed that my mother, when washing my clothes with a blue, cube soap for brightening, had also added too much starch, which stiffened my clothing, thus causing me to feel uncomfortable. When I asked them if I could wear my shirt outside my pants, both of them said no.

Minutes later when my grandmother saw me constantly adjusting my clothes, she said, "Why yuh look so fidgety? Stop titivatin' wid yuh shut like if yuh gat stingin' nettles!" With me not allowed to wear my shirt outside my pants and her telling me that I was restless, I got angry and yelled, "Ajee, don't hambug meh! Lef meh alone! Yuh crampin' meh style!" Even though I requested that they stop fussing over me, and not get in my way of dressing, they insisted that I wear my shirt tucked into my pants.

Believing that the clothes I had on were the best clothing I had at the time, I was hopeful that by noon, when I perspired from the heat of the sun, my clothes would become softer. Finally, when it was time to leave, my grandmother noticed that one of the laces on my sneakers had come loose. She affectionately said, "Come beta, leh meh tie yuh yaatin boots." After tying my laces, she flattered me once more about how good I looked when she softly said, "Yuh look like ah real sweet boy, come leh meh hug yuh!"

My journey to Leguan was an unforgettable experience on a ship called the Malali. I clearly remember standing aloof and looking at two men direct the drivers of cars as they came onto the ship. I watched with intense interest how vehicles had to cross on two narrow pieces of sturdy wood to get from the dock onto the ship. It worried me that if a driver made a fatal mistake when boarding, his vehicle could accidentally tumble into the deep river. I recall my mother saying on this journey that the large river we were sailing on was called the Essequibo River, which was said to be the longest river in Guyana.

Arriving in Leguan, my grandmother (nani) was the first person to greet my mother and me. Shortly after she gave me a big hug, I was surprised when she untied a knot on one end of her frock (dress) and gave me a penny. Though I was thankful for her gift, I was somewhat puzzled by where she kept her money.

Minutes later, I was introduced to my mother's sister Aunty Nelly and ten of her children. The moment my aunt saw me she gave a broad smile and asked if I was thirsty. Hearing me say yes, she went into the kitchen and quickly brought me a cup of a homemade drink called "swank," which was a mixture of water, sugar and lime.

I was delighted when I saw Aunty Nelly for she was a generous person who always brought me a "shugah cake" and a small bunch of bananas, called "sweet figs," whenever she came to visit us in Georgetown. Meeting her on this occasion, I noticed that she was not overweight as I had seen her over the years. I came to realize that she was not a fat person, but because she was pregnant almost every year, I assumed she was overweight.

As I stood beneath my grandmother's home, which was supported on solid posts about six feet high, I was in awe to see how smooth and clean the area under the house looked. When I inquired from my grandmother how the earth we stood on was so smooth, she told me that they "daab de battam house" with a mixture of cow manure and mud.

As I curiously looked around, I saw a man "lall-aff"

(relaxing) in a hammock with his eyes closed, but before I could inquire who he was, my grandmother told me he was Aunty Nelly's husband Sam. When Uncle Sam heard my grandmother's voice, he suddenly woke up, looking rather surprised to see me. Seeing him with his shirt open and the black hairs on his chest glistening with perspiration from the hot sun, I assumed that he was taking a five-minute nap in the gentle breeze that was blowing. As a show of respect I said to him, "Mornin' Uncle Sam, like yuh tekkin' a five or yuh tekkin' breeze?" But he looked somewhat annoyed and grumpily said, "Yuh look like wan saga bai! Meh could tell yuh come from town!" With him not smiling and saying I looked flashy and came from the city, I could not tell if he was making fun of me. It was not until he opened his big mouth and asked if I knew the difference between people of the countryside and those from Georgetown that I came to think he was arrogant.

When I said to Uncle Sam that I did not know the answer to his question, he smirked and said that when people of the city went to visit relatives living in the countryside, they always showed up empty-handed, meaning they had nothing to offer. But when people from the countryside went to visit relatives in Georgetown, they always took something for them to eat. Being taught from a tender age that I had to be respectful to my elders, I remained silent and did not say anything to agitate him. As I was about to walk away, Uncle Sam softly said, "Bai nah tek meh serious, meh ah only tantalize yuh." Though he told me not to take him seriously and claimed that he was only teasing me, I was still unhappy with the question he had asked me. However, rethinking matters, it seemed that there was an element of truth about what he was saying, for whenever my grandmother or Aunty Nelly came to visit us in Georgetown, they always brought us a couple of chickens, some rice and "sweet fig" bananas.

Later in the day, when the sun was about to set,

Aunty Nelly lit a bottle lamp before calling out to five of her ten children to get seated on the floor, as it was dinnertime. She then told me to sit on a "peerha," (stool) saying that I would be comfortable on it. My aunt then gave each of her five older children a plate of rice and a piece of curried fish called "hoorie." I thought that I was going to get the same as them, but instead, she gave each of her five younger children and me a bowl of rice with milk and sugar added to it. Not pleased with the food that was given to me, I questioned my aunt why I could not have the rice with fish. She politely replied that the fish had plenty of bones, and seeing that I had not eaten that particular fish before, she was afraid that the bones might get suck in my throat.

After serving dinner, Aunty Nelly took the lamp to another area of the house where my mother was seated to talk "ol' time story" (chat) with her. I was puzzled when my aunt left her children and me to eat in partial darkness, as I could not comprehend how her older children could eat the fish with plenty of bones in the dark. After eating, I quietly got up and looked through a window to see all the neighboring houses in darkness, drawing me to think that there was no electricity in the area.

Early the following morning, I saw Aunty Nelly gathering pieces of wood. When I asked her the reason she replied, "Abee ah guh cook!" When she indicated that more than one person would be cooking, I went into the kitchen to see who would be assisting her, and saw my mother pouring flour into a bowl and my grandmother cutting up vegetables.

It was interesting to see Aunty Nelly use a "fiyah side" (mud stove) to cook on. I looked with intense interest when my grandmother said, "Gyal, gyam fire!", and my aunt took out a pipe many called a "pookney" and began blowing the coals in the fireside to increase the fire. Seeing this reminded me of an earlier period when my parents had a fireside, and then one day it was removed from our house and replaced with a kerosene stove.

Finally, when breakfast was served, my aunt's children and I got a hearty meal of sadha roti, baigan chokah (roasted eggplant), salt fish cakes, as well as some warm milk served in an enamel cup. It turned out to be a little amusing while eating, that one of Aunty Nelly's sons appeared displeased with his food and loudly said, "Ma, yuh gime bun bun roti fuh eat!" With him saying that parts of the roti he was eating were burnt, his mother told him to take off what was bad and to eat the rest of it. Amid it all, I had to smile when one of Aunty Nelly's daughters told her brother not to complain about his food, and if he didn't want it to give it to her.

As I observed my Aunty Nelly, who after breakfast began cleaning the yard, it seemed to me that her daily tasks were to clean the house, prepare meals and make babies. I must say that for someone with ten children, she looked about thirty-two years of age. I could only guess that she was one of a number of young women of her time who got married at age sixteen. Listening to her occasionally complain to my grandmother about the number of chores she had to do, I was surprised when my grandmother declared that she had more chores to do when she was a young woman than Aunty Nelly. My grandmother made it clear that apart from raising many children, she had to cut grass, tend to cows and work long hours in the rice fields.

Later in the day my aunt's eldest son, who was about two years older than me, mentioned that he had a few errands to do and would come back in an hour's time to play with me. I was surprised to see him taking a container of milk on a bicycle to sell to people in the surrounding area. When he returned from selling milk, I realized that he was more mature than me, for he not only shared the responsibility with his parents to take care of his younger brothers and sisters, but he even knew how to milk cows, plant rice and chop coconuts with a cutlass. Seeing that my cousin could ride a bike, I politely asked him to teach me to ride. I remember spending almost two hours learning to ride on a dirt road, but unfortunately it was not enough time for me to ride properly.

Early the next morning, my mother took me by surprise when she informed me that in a couple of hours we would be leaving to go back to Georgetown, as she had to return home to take care of my sister and two brothers who were left with my father. It saddened me to leave so soon, as I was beginning to get more acquainted with my relatives in Leguan.

Finally, it was time to depart, and it was pleasing to see my grandmother giving my mother a gallon of rice and a couple of chickens to take home. I was even more delighted when my grandmother softly said, "Come beta, come fah wan jill," meaning that I should come to her for a penny, which she took out from the knot on her dress.

Arriving in Georgetown at a central marketplace called Stabroek that was bustling with activity, my mother asked me if I was hungry. Nodding my head to say yes, she then took me to a shop inside the market and bought me a tasty drink called "peanut punch" and a red-colored coconut cake called "salara." Like most children who enjoyed tasty things, I was delighted with what my mother bought me as I ate all of it to the last crumb.

After eating, my mother took the opportunity to take me to see a famous wooden building called the St. George's Cathedral, and two major shopping stores named Fogarty's and Bookers. I must say that it was a strenuous walk for my mother, as she had to carry around the bag that had the two chickens and the rice that we brought from Leguan. Seeing the two shopping stores fascinated me, as they carried a wide variety of toys, clothing and shoes that I wished to have.

As we ambled along the sidewalk, my mother and I were surprised to see a crowd of people standing in front of a building. Curious to see what was happening, we moved closer to the crowd. As I eased my way through people, I was astonished to see a man holding up a doll with a string around its neck, and commenting about the law and the evil things that people did. Listening to this man speak with a commanding voice, and pretend that he was passing judgment and executing someone, I asked my mother who he was. I was surprised when she told me that people nicknamed him "Law and Order." She then said to me that this man had some form of mental illness and what he was saying was not important. I must say that my trip to the downtown area was brief, for after seeing "Law and Order," my mother looking somewhat tired, said it was time to leave.

Soon we got ready to board a big, yellow bus; however, I became unlucky when my mother, carrying the heavy bag in her hands, used her hip to push the turnstile on the bus, and with me following close behind, the arm of the turnstile flew back and hit me on my chin. As I placed my hands on it and began to cry, my mother said she was sorry and urged me to stop. However, it was not until she told me that if I stopped crying she would buy me a glass of freshly squeezed "cane juice" when we got closer to home that I dried my tears and stopped crying.

When the bus took off it sounded noisy as though it were old; however, I was pleased that it was not crowded. Seeing that it was not full, my mother allowed me to sit by myself towards the rear of the bus so that I could get a good view of the downtown area. As I moved freely on the seat to see various stores, this freedom suddenly halted when a man who had just got on the bus came next to me and rudely said, "Shif' yuh carcass!," meaning that I should move over to make room for him to sit. When this stranger plopped down next to me, he made me angry when he bumped my hip. Believing that he had done it intentionally, I said, "Don't shub meh!" But when I said that he angrily replied, "Whey yuh seh?" With him rudely asking what I said, I remained silent and did not say anything to further agitate him.

While sitting by the window, I got up from my seat to look through the glass at a policeman riding a horse; however, I was left astonished when the man next to me crossly said, "Yuh fadda is ah glassmaker?" Meaning that I was blocking his view through the window, I decided to move to the front of the bus to sit next to my mother.

Returning home about thirty minutes later, I was eager to tell my cousins about my trip to Leguan. However, while talking to them I saw a bus filled with people draw to a halt in front of our house. I learned that most of them were my father's relatives, who had come from the countryside to pick up two of my uncles to attend a cricket match between Australia and the West Indies at a ground called Bourda. As I watched them get off the bus one by one, I recognized a woman whom I had seen a year ago when she came to visit my grandparents. I must say that I was happy to see her, and as a show of respect I politely said, "Hi antie!" Looking at me, she gave a big smile and replied, "Oh meh muhma! Bai, yuh know meh to ah 'T' Come leh meh hise yuh!" With her telling me that I knew her well, and asking that I come to her so that she could lift me up with affection, I honestly felt that she really liked me. As I silently pondered on what to say to her, I was taken aback when she said, "Bai yuh look magah! Tek dis cent and put it in yuh puzzlin' tin!" Listening to her telling me that I was skinny and only offering me one cent to put in my piggy bank, I felt displeased. Seeing her with a lot of jewelry around her neck and on one of her wrists, I thought she was rich, hence I begged her to give me five cents. Suddenly, she became annoyed and said, "Look bai! Nah badda meh! Gwhan dah side!" With her telling me not to bother her and to go away, I looked at her crossly. But she became furious and pointed her finger at me before harshly saying, "Nah cut yuh eye pon meh, befuh abe fall out!" Realizing that she was not pleased when I cast a glaring eye at her, I decided to walk away before she complained to my grandmother that I was rude.

Seeing one of my uncles putting on his shoes to leave home, I decided to plead with him to take me to watch the cricket game. However, he repeatedly told me that everyone on the bus was an adult and I could not go with them. It was not until he angrily said, "Yuh like pat salt! Yuh see how rum bottles does pack, lil from big, eh?" that I got the message that I could not be in everything, and he did not want to have me in the company of adults.

A few hours later, I was astonished when I saw the entire busload of people return to our house, looking rather unhappy. After enquiring why they came back so soon, I learned that they all went to see the famous cricketer Rohan Kanhai and were disappointed when Kanhai made a poor score.

While our guests chatted, my uncle gave me some money to purchase a bottle of White Rum, a few bottles of Coca-Cola and some ice. However, about twenty minutes later when I returned with the items, my uncle realized after I had left that it would not be convenient to have so many people in our house. He then decided to take the liquor back to the rum shop where I bought it and to drink it there instead with most of the male guests.

What I found amusing this day was that a few blocks away from the rum shop was an area where a number of young men had gathered around to climb a post that was covered in grease and extended about twenty-two feet above the ground. This post, called a "greasy pole," had a bottle of rum at the top. It turned out to be hilarious when one of my uncle's friends, who was drunk, took off his pants and began to climb the slippery pole. While he made a fool of himself, struggling to climb it, others had a hearty laugh. I clearly remember that on that day no one was successful in climbing the pole. It took days for someone who was determined to accomplish this feat to take the prize of a bottle of rum.

Days later, while playing in our yard, I noticed that my uncle's bicycle under the stairs of our house was unlocked. Seeing that he was not at home, I decided to take his bike for a ride without his permission. While moving the bike, I noticed that it had no brakes; however, I was determined to ride it. But just as I was about to get started, a friend of mine nicknamed Tallboy, seeing me with the bike, shouted, "Bai, weh yuh geh da chubang from?" With him asking where I got the bike from, I told him not to speak so loud and we would take turns to ride it. Being the first to go, I managed after a few failed attempts to keep control of the bike. However, while riding a little faster, I suddenly realized that with no brakes, I had to come up with some other means of stopping. Seeing a street light post in the distance, I decided to ride close to it and quickly grab onto the post to stop. Unfortunately, this was not a wise thing to do for while grabbing onto the post, I got badly bruised on my upper arm. Realizing that this was a bad idea, I decided to try something new to stop the bike when riding. On this occasion, I decided after riding a fairly good distance to go across a small heap of sand, but unfortunately the bike wobbled and I tumbled, striking my head on the ground. About thirty seconds later, Tallboy hurriedly came to the scene saying, "Oh skites bai! Yuh look bazadee! Ah fahget fuh tell yuh, nah fuh ride pon san." With him saying that I looked confused and he had forgotten to tell me not to ride on sand, I gave him a fierce look.

Seeing me in pain and rubbing the side of my head, Tallboy said, "Bai, bear yuh chafe, yuh betta go home an' leh yuh mudda sapp yuh head wid Limacol." With him advising me to show some courage by not flinching, and to go home and get my head rubbed with a refreshing lotion called Limacol, I decided to take his advice. Unfortunately, from the moment I entered our yard, my grandmother, seeing me with the bike, angrily said, "Picknee, yuh prappa bad! Nah mek meh geh in meh rickaticks! Put dah bike back weh yuh find it!" With her telling me not to make her get enraged and for me to put back the bike where I found it, I hurriedly did what she requested.

*****

As I reflect on some of my boyhood experiences in 1964, they sometimes bring back happy memories of those I loved, and with whom I was fortunate to share some of the simple joys in life. One thing that made me unhappy in 1964 was when I observed for the first time many of my relatives and our neighbors leaving Guyana to go to either England or America. I remember asking many adults why they were leaving, but sadly they did not tell me why, declaring they were only going on a holiday, and I shouldn't be so inquisitive. I must say they were untrue to me for by the time I reached age fifteen, none of them came back to live in Guyana.

Departing from Guyana to go to a foreign nation was a memorable moment in the lives of many, as carloads of relatives and friends would accompany those who were leaving for the airport. What touched me the most when going to the airport for the first time was to see so many embrace their relatives who were departing and tearfully say goodbye. With so many people lamenting, it seemed that those who were going abroad would be greatly missed, and would be spending many years away from home. To show how closely knitted some families were, I recall that whenever my grandfather got a letter from overseas, everyone was so happy to hear what the relative abroad had to say, that they would all gather around to hear him read the letter.

*****

After I became thirteen years of age, my parents enrolled me in a private high school where I met a number of students who came from neighboring villages. My classroom was very large as there were seventy-three students in our class.

On the first day at school, I was told by the principal to sit next to a girl until proper seating arrangements were made for some of us. Sitting beside this beautiful girl, I could not help smiling when a boy who was passing by cheerfully said, "Bai, like yuh ketch t'ing?" hinting that I got a nice girl friend.

Attending high school was a challenging experience for many of us, as it was common to see students getting lashes on the palms of their hands or on their buttocks for giving the wrong answers to questions. While some boys flinched when they got spanked on their buttocks, others who stuffed a piece of cloth or paper in their underwear to cushion the blow pretended it was painful.

After a few weeks in school, I discovered that most of the students in my class were very smart and took their education seriously. In the beginning, I was playful and not quite focused on what was taught in school, but with time, I developed a strong interest in History and the English language. While I was keen about learning the history of my country, I was also interested in reading about the political problems in many foreign nations. A year after the war in Vietnam started, it became a habit for me to listen to the BBC news daily, which informed listeners about the unleashing of bombs and the number of soldiers killed. I became so wrapped up in current and past events that I often borrowed many adult books to read about the atrocities that were committed by many dictators.

Within months at school I became friends with two boys who often talked about some of the great movies they saw. One day, they began to encourage me to "scult" (skip school) to see a popular "picha" (movie) called "One Silver Dollar" staring the famous Italian actor Giuliano Gemma who in the coming years became my favorite movie star. At the time it was difficult for me to say no to my good friends who were trying to convince me to go with them. Rethinking matters, I told them to go ahead with their plans and I would remain silent about it. Unfortunately for them, someone reported to the principal that two students wearing the uniform of our school were seen in the cinema. I remember seeing the principal of my school about 2:00 p.m. that day, bringing my two friends into our classroom, announcing to everyone that he had gone into the cinema and found them. The principal then gave each of them four lashes on their buttocks, and told them that when they returned home in the evening to tell their parents about the wrong they had done.

After my friends were punished, the principal gave a brief talk to the entire class. In his speech I clearly remember him saying that most of us came from poor families, and if any of us failed our exams it would be a huge disappointment for our parents who did menial work to pay our school fees. What he said immediately made me reflect on the struggles of my own parents.

Age fourteen marked a new phase in my life, as I began to think through matters that were of concern to me. Though I had an interest in politics, as well as spiritual beliefs, I was not easily influenced by the ideas of politicians or preachers who tried to convince me to follow their footsteps. Although I was a happy-go-lucky person, my mindset as a teen was to think rationally and to follow what my conscience told me was right. Aside from this, the type of music that I listened to as a teenager somewhat contributed to the shaping of my personality. I became a fan of the British soft rock singer Cliff Richards and from listening to thoughtful lyrics, I developed affectionate feelings for my loved ones.

*****

At age fifteen my grandfather passed away and it became a period of great sadness for my relatives. I recall, about 7:30 p.m. on the day my grandfather died, being asked by my grandmother to go with one of my cousins, who was a year older than me, to a funeral home. We were told to tell the owner, who knew my grandfather well, that he had passed away and for him to arrange a coffin.

Arriving at the main entrance of the funeral home that night, we found the place in darkness and no one in sight. Pondering on what to do, my cousin suggested that we go towards the rear of the building where coffins were kept. As we passed through an area that was fairly dark my cousin, looking somewhat bewildered, quietly said, "Bai, yuh know weh we deh?" After he asked if I knew where we were, I felt a bit at ease when I saw a light in the distance. As we cautiously approached the light, my heart pounded with fear when a man who was lying in a coffin slowly sat up and asked, "Who allyuh lookin' fuh?" With him being the person who made coffins and not the owner, asking who we were looking for, I decided to tell him that my grandfather had passed away and my grandmother wanted to order a coffin for him. When I mentioned the name of my grandfather, the man immediately expressed his sympathy. He was kind and told us not to worry for he would have a coffin ready for us the following day. I then gave him the message that one of my relatives would be coming the next day to pay for the funeral expenses.

At home it was sad to see so many relatives weeping

in grief. As I stood next to my grandmother, I was puzzled when she was asked by a few sympathizers what was the cause of death of my grandfather, and she sadly replied, "E tekin' an' e dead." With her saying that he got sick and died, I could only guess that my grandfather died a natural death. Later that night, I became puzzled when one of my aunts, who was very superstitious, suggested that someone tie the big toes of the deceased together, fearing that the dead man would walk back to our home after the funeral.

The following day one of my relatives went to meet a popular individual in our area named Joe Taylor. This man, who was of Afro-Guyanese descent, was paid a small fee to announce the death of my grandfather. I clearly remember Joe riding a bicycle and sounding a bell through various streets, saying publicly that my grandfather had died and the time he would be buried. Apart from announcing the demise of people in our area, Joe was well-known for playing the "tassa" drums at many Hindu marriage ceremonies. I must say that at that time, he was considered one of the best "tassa" players in the country.

During the festive season at Christmas, it was common to see Joe wearing a traditional men's garment of India called "dhoti kurta" and carrying a long stick. Though he was greatly respected by many adults, I could not say the same for many children, who liked to tease him when he sang and danced. To get on Joe's nerves, some children called him "Dead Snake." It was hilarious for many to see Joe Taylor, annoyed when called by that name, chasing a group of children down the road to scare them away.

*****

In Guyana it was customary that whenever friends

or relatives came to visit, people usually offered them cooked food or something to drink. I must say that the Guyanese hospitality was pleasing to many who visited Guyana from distant lands, for they often spoke to others about it. I remember from a tender age, when visiting my friends, how their parents would invite me into their homes to offer me a fruit or something to eat.

Most Guyanese abroad are generous to their relatives at home, for even though many emigrated to foreign lands, you can hear some say, "Ah gah fuh sen' ah small piece fuh meh family back home." This caring feeling of wanting to send a little money for their relatives in Guyana is what I witnessed as a boy, for I recall my relatives abroad occasionally sending money or gifts to my grandparents to distribute to others.

Now that I am fifteen years of age, I am drawn to think how fortunate I was to be born in a nation like Guyana, as the people who live there love life, they love music, they love friends, and the game of cricket helps to maintain unity among people of the Caribbean, especially when the West Indies cricket team plays against a foreign nation. Though I have not traveled to some of the most beautiful regions of Guyana such as the Pakaraima Mountains, the dry grasslands of the Rupununi, the rainforest and the Kaieteur Falls, it is my wish to visit these places when I become an adult.

With today being a bright, sunny day in the month of October 1968, it fills my heart with joy when my friends of Portuguese, Chinese and Afro-Guyanese descent come to where I live, asking that I join them in playing our favorite game, cricket. On some evenings it is common for many of us teens to "lime" (hang-out) at the corner of a particular street, or in the yard where a friend lives, to talk about sports, music, school, and even to joke around or talk about things we find amusing. Though we're of different races and call one another by nicknames, we tend not to harbor hatred or quarrel over religious beliefs. Having these friends that I grew up with from a tender age, my only wish is that we remain united and not become too sensitive in the distant future, and not take offence if one were to say "Merry Christmas." It is also my wish that the people of Guyana remain united and not allow themselves to become divided by those who incite trouble, and like to stir up people's emotions by making racism an issue. The thing that worries me at times is why so many people are leaving Guyana to go abroad after it has gained independence. Being a teenager who sometimes feels left out when many in our village refuse to tell me why they are leaving, I can only assume that there is a growing uncertainty about the future of our nation. I must say that amid it all, I am hopeful that the future of Guyana will be bright, for I honestly believe that there are people who sincerely care about our nation and would like to see it prosper.

I remember meeting an uncle who came from abroad, and he said to me that the vast majority of Guyanese who have emigrated to foreign lands have done exceptionally well, and we should all be proud that for a country with a population of about seven hundred and fifty thousand people, Guyana has produced a very high number of educated people. Listening to what he said made me proud; hence it is my wish as a fifteen-year-old boy for Guyana to strive in leaps and bounds to reach the summit of maturity, and for it to rest there in an abode of peace and prosperity.

**List of Short Stories by J.R. Singh:**
The True Self
Cryonic Man

**Pandora's Heartaches**
An Afterlife Dream
Lessons of Marriage
The Fragility of Life
A Sage's Dream
Turbulent Minds
Tyranny and Freedom
Nammu's Abode
My Children Bring Joy and Pain
Disloyalty and Revenge
Changes in Life
Acts of Terror
How Attitudes Change
The Sons of Ivan Hayley
Survival

**Strange Misfortunes**
Wolves in Priestly Clothing
Leaders and Followers
The Dream of a Prophet
Even Soldiers Have Hearts
An Edifying Dream About a Tyrant

**The Tolerance of Hinduism**

**Adventures of the Homeless** (novel)

**List of Essays by J.R. Singh:**

**Earthly Tribulations**
Corrupt Governments
Personality
Spiritual Beliefs
War
Racism
Women's Rights
Abortion
Laws
Television and the Media
Health Care
Nature
Mind and Body
Sickness and Death
Life after Death
Poverty

**Children Stories by J.R. Singh**
Careless Willy
Puppy Joe
Chubby George

**Website:** http://www.jagdishraisingh.com